The World of White Water

The World of White Water

Poems by

Willy Conley

Cover design by Shay Culligan
Cover photo by Willy Conley

ISBN: 978-1-63980-036-0

Kelsay Books
502 South 1040 East, A-119
American Fork, Utah 84003
Kelsaybooks.com

For my mother, Katharine Louisa

Acknowledgments

I gratefully acknowledge the editors and publishers of the following publications in which these poems first appeared:

Deaf American Poetry: "A Deaf Baptism," "Salt in the Basement," "The Miller of Moments"

The Deaf Way II Anthology: "The Cycle of the X-Ray Technician," "Salt in the Basement," "The Perfect Woman"

TYA Today: "The Universal Drum"

The Washington Post: "The Honeybee Epiphany." (originally "Autobiography as Haiku")

No Walls of Stone: "One Frame at a Time" (originally "One Frame Per Second")

OVS Magazine: "A Maryland Eastern Shore Life"

ICON: "November Rust," "Someone's Daughter," "I of the Beholder"

Modern Haiku: "Coyote Bones"

The Tactile Mind: "The water falls."

Deaf Lit Extravaganza: "The Ivoryton Inn"

the Newer York!: "We Don't Do Voiceovers: A Deaf Man's Muses to-Do List" (originally "We Don't Do Voiceovers: A Deaf Man Muses")

Special thanks

The Bethesda Academy of Performing Arts' Imagination Stage commissioned the writing of "The Universal Drum" as a performance piece for the Deaf Access Company in 2002.

I am incredibly grateful to Helen Frost for her organic, insightful feedback on this collection.

I wish to thank my past and present teachers, who have instilled a sense of poetry no matter how great or small, Derek Walcott, Natalie Goldberg, Alexa Selph, Juanita Rockwell, David Hays, Robert Panara, Loy Golladay, Patrick Graybill, Sam Abrams, Stephen Policoff, Anne Greene, Pia Taavila, Kim Peter Kovac, James Selby, Shanny Mow, Perry & Kitty Conley—my parents, and always, my son Clayton.

And, to Ingrid Weidner for reading, "listening," and offering—danke!

Contents

"The water you touch in a river is the last of that which has gone, and the first of that which is coming…"
—Leonardo da Vinci, *Thoughts on Art and Life*

I. The Rapids

A Deaf Baptism

A family of mallards
by a waterfall's green ledge
paddling
preening
shivering off water bugs.
A feather or two comes loose
and floats over the water's edge.

Suddenly a duckling
chasing after a feather
flapping
jerking
toppling over the waterfall.
Lost, it struggles through
the curtain into the world of white water.

Salt in the Basement

—An American Sign Language reverie in English

happen summer
me little, almost high wash-wash machine
down basement, me have blue car
drive drive round round
basement

me drive every corner
drive drive drive
then BOOM! me crash

there tall paper brown round
me get out car
look inside brown round tall
many many small small
white rock rock
small white rock rock

for-for?

me put white rock rock
in mouth
very very salty
same-same Grandma
mashed-mashed potato

me back inside blue car
drive drive round round
basement

happen winter
father down basement
go to brown round tall
father shovel big lump

there white rock rock
many white rock rock

father told me for-for
outside road

me ask again for-for?
me outside blue car, cold cold
drive drive straight straight
me watch father

white rock rock father throw throw
on walk-walk
father his brown car
throw white rock rock
throw round throw round

me ask father for-for?

father say for mother
white rock rock for mother?

me get out blue car
me look down white rock rock
burn burn hole many many
hole in ice
same-same ice in my lemonade

me jaw-drop
white rock rock rock
make hole in ice break-break
same-same make hole in my tummy?

that why me pee-pee
poo-poo always?

me no more eat
white rock rock
inside basement

me remember
mother year last
happen winter
mother outside
ice all-over
mother fall
arm broke

father told me
go down basement
stay stay
me inside blue car
drive round round
basement

The Deaf Delivery Boy

He brought home a picture from first grade:
a line-drawn man of pumpkins.

For homework he colored it purple.
Teacher wrote on his drawing:
"A PURPLE PUMPKIN MAN??"

Father seethed and wrote
in bigger letters saying:
"A <u>PUMPKIN</u> MAN???"

Once again the boy carried
the drawing back to the teacher.

The Galvanic Skin Response Test

(a bilingual memory in American Sign Language recollection and English expression)

age 4
me in hospital
doctor electric wires
tape tape tape
face, arms, legs

long, long spaghetti wires
to machine
connect, connect, connect

earphones over-my-head
feel-same vise (twist, twist, twist)
pressure-lock

red button
doctor finger press
suddenly
electric shocks
like rug me walk walk
touch doorknob
lightning sssssizzle!

Me jump out
but doctor grabs me back
WHUMP! on seat
spaghetti wires everywhere

Then machine tongue out
long thin paper
blue lines
fast up-and-down-
up-and-down-up-and-down…

Doctor head nods
he pats my leg
then rip, rip, rip
off tape
legs, arms, face
my eyes water fill
thought he tore off
my skin

The Honeybee Epiphany

An autumn afternoon in first grade.
I felt a tickle behind my ear,
brushed it away. I must have yelped
because my teacher rushed over
and pointed to a honeybee on the floor.
I didn't understand. She gestured
for me to take out my "things."
I pulled out my hearing aids,
which emitted high-pitched feedback.
Everyone stared while she coated my ear
with baking soda. I looked at the dying bee,
not realizing that moment
would be the beginning
of many years of jeers
about my deafness.

Assimilating in the Hearing World

Three boys sit together
on a sofa in a den
watching an afternoon soap:
Dark Shadows.

The deaf one,
left out of conversation
and plot line
(no closed-captioning in the '70s),
sits on the end.

He takes in the scene:
a man's canines grow long
and sink into the necks
of unsuspecting people.

The hearing boy next to him bites
into some Saltines but won't swallow.
He drains all the saliva out of his mouth,
compacts the cracker pieces,
and takes out a cracker ball.

Then he takes little
squirrel bites out of it.

Meanwhile, the hearing boy
at the other end
unzips his pants
to show off his thing.

Tween Dilemma

In Austria, deaf people actually have
a government card identifying them
as disabled.

Twelve at the time,
she went with her mother
to look for a Christmas tree.
They pointed out one they liked
to the vendor.

Before paying, her mother
pulled out the Deaf Card
to elicit a discount.
The daughter hid her face
walking away.
Her mother grabbed her,
turned her around, and signed:

"Do you want to give that hearing man
the full price or ask for a reduced cost
and use what's leftover
for candy and ice cream?"

Mr. Bowersox

the substitute math teacher for the day
at Southern High
is a white, slow-moving, 90-year-old,
severely hard-of-hearing man
with a screechy voice.

It takes him 15 minutes to do roll call
for he can't correctly pronounce many
of the ethnic-sounding names.
When time to hand out an assignment,
someone bold enough to speak up and lie, said:
"We already did that, Mr. Bowersox."

"Oh, okay," he said. And then
the students were free to chat
for the remainder of the class as
Mr. Bowersox sat there, reshuffling
the handouts, pleased they knew his name
and probably speaking highly of him.

Deaf/th Metaphysics

silence

never existed

there's always sound

audible

       or imaginary

say silence exists

means life ends

after death

       one thing for certain

hearing people often

misspeak death

       for deaf

Speechless

Funny,youdon'tlookdeaf.Doyoureallyneed
aninterpreter?Areclosed-captionsreally
necessary?Howcanyoulivewithout
music?Areyourothersensesheightened?
CanyoureadBraille?Howdoyouwakeup
inthemorning?Howcanyoudrive
ifyoucan'thear?Whynotgetacochlearimplant
oreartransplant?Youdon'tsounddeaf.Youspeak
prettygoodforsomeonewho'sdeaf.

Never mind, not important.

The Ivoryton Inn

—in memory of Dorothy Miles

Empty bar at the Ivoryton Inn
just the bartender, me, and the TV.
The odor of stale cigarette smoke
and beer clings to everything made of wood.
This is the town where they used to ship elephant tusks
up the river and forge them into piano keys.

He's skinny with sunken cheeks, deep-set eyes.
All he wears is black. He tries to strike
a conversation but I hear nothing; I only
see mumbling lips and CNN
on the tube in the background.

I just nod.

Though no one has come in,
he constantly wipes the bar.
I order a glass of wine, and when it comes,
I make sure the glass stays
on the coaster.

I lived upstairs in this place
two summers past to interview deaf theater students
from the world over. They came to this bar
to eat, drink, and rehearse play scenes
for the drama school held in an
old, renovated grist mill nearby.

Their silhouettes sit beside me, and
some with drinks in their hands
lean on the baby grand piano:

Shan from Hong Kong complains
about the lack of opportunity
for deaf actors in his country.
Anu from India isn't here to learn
about acting but ways to meet American men
and get a green card.

Loretta, the redhead, from Australia—
unaware that she has no stage presence—
thinks her flashy personality will attract all
sorts of Hollywood offers.

Tom from England studies a Pinter monologue
and drinks milk; he tries out words in
two-handed British fingerspelling.

As if it were just yesterday,
I see their facial expressions and
native sign languages,
each with its own signature and syntax.

In the early seventies
a deaf theater company won a Tony Award.
A sudden growing interest
in hiring deaf actors came about.
Hundreds and hundreds of eager deaf students
enrolled in the summer program
each one manufactured—
some against their will—
to the specs of well-known acting teachers
and directors from New York City who could hear.

I finish my wine and leave a tip
at the bar's edge. The bartender
gives me a shifty glance and then
swoops in like a vulture to grab his
money and put the wine glass away.
He wipes the entire bar again, even
though only a small area was smudged.

On the way out I touch the baby grand.
My hand trails along the curves,
stopping at the keyboard.

I strike a black key, an unknown note,
thinking about fabricated deaf actors.
I tap a white key and wonder about
the elephants in Africa or India
or wherever they were caught.

What were these humble creatures
feeling when the poachers held them down
to saw off their noble tusks?

The Miller of Moments

On Pattaconk Brook
in Chester, Connecticut,
up in a little tower
above the old grist mill

someone
steams rain
sifts thunder
sews lightning
squeezes sunlight
saves sign language

a pair of hands
opens the wood slats

the flowers hold their scents
the brook ceases babbling
the ivy stops crawling
the wind looks back

eyes for darkness
watch below
the daily struts and frets
of drama school deaf actors
their private moments

when the sun
bows to the horizon
the hands withdraw

come morning the summer school cook
rips yesterday off the calendar
before people walk in and out
for three squares a day

no one notices
the yearly scores
of faint footprints
up on the mill tower deck

yet another day
the spirit of deaf theater
survives

A Meditation on Natural Gestures

(English translation of American Sign Language on Film)

Without wind I sway with wild *sea oats*
No clay in hand, I build a *brick* wall
From a sidewalk impression I take out a shivering *leaf*
In a fireplace my fingers add *flame* to wood
At a park bench, a *sandwich* materializes in my hands
By the river under the Thomas Viaduct
I watch *my body* cross the bridge
before the train comes
—all done by shaping air
with my *hands*

The Cycle of the X-Ray Technician

Whenever I feel down about my deafness,
my receding hairline, my weight,
my glaucoma, and on and on, I remind myself—
the X-ray Technician.

I passed him every time I delivered
some files to Medical Records.
He'd hang up recently processed X-rays
on the light boxes with the blue light
illuminating a badly burned and disfigured face—
the X-ray Technician.

He had one normal arm,
the other a prosthesis with a metal claw.
I'd start to feel sorry for him…
then I stopped myself.
I wouldn't want him to pity me—
the X-ray Technician.

For all I know, he may have his own home
with a beautiful wife, lover, or family.
He may be an excellent artist
or a freelance auto mechanic.
He may be the best bowler in Texas
or have the highest RBI on his softball team
or, he may be lonely,
feeling sorry for himself like me—
the X-ray Technician.

We Don't Do Voiceovers: A Deaf Man's Muses-to-Do List

- If a deaf person has to go to court, is it still called a hearing?
- "Dialogue of the deaf"—why do hearing people keep saying that? It makes no sense. You should see my deaf friends sign with each other in dialogue all day long till the cows come home.
- "Fall on deaf ears"—there was once a play, by a Deaf playwright, called *Falling on Hearing Eyes—a museum of sign /anguish for people with communication disorders.* It was mostly about people who could hear but couldn't communicate.
- "Stone deaf"—this one is a proud label for many of my deaf peers. The deafer they are, the prouder.
- Do farts smell so deaf people can enjoy them too?
- Morning announcement at a high school before a stage performance by a mixed group of deaf and hearing actors (interpreted by one of the hearing actors):
   "We have a special assembly for all of you today presenting a deaf-mute choral group."
- Referring to my behind-the-ear hearing aids, a woman in a restaurant leaned over and asked: "Do those things in your ears really help you lose weight?"
- A conversation between one of my co-workers and her daughter:
   Candy: I know how he does it, Mommy. I know how he lipreads.
   Mommy: How?
   Candy: Saw a football player on TV. This is what he said: (she mouths the word) "asshole."
- Take the couple with an ever-growing family of 11 children. The husband explained that this was because his wife was hard-of-hearing. Every night when they went to bed, the husband would ask, "Do you want to go to sleep or what?"
   "What?" his wife answered.
- A profoundly deaf friend had her tonsils removed at an early age because doctors thought that it would help her hear.

- During one Christmas, my aunt gave me *A Wild and Crazy Guy,* a double-album of Steve Martin's standup comedy routines. I was still in college when I received it. That means that at the age of 23, my own aunt still couldn't conceive of the idea that I was profoundly deaf.
- At a McDonald's restaurant, a Deaf friend, who doesn't speak, gestured to the clerk that he was deaf, and would like a picture menu to point out his choices for ordering lunch. The clerk handed him a Braille menu.
- Seen on the brown wrapper of a part for assembling a mailbox: "Contents of this bag have been packaged by the blind and the handicapped." Whoopee-fucking-do! Yes, people with disabilities work and are productive members of society. Why does that need to be broadcasted on a bag?
- Deaf people don't do voiceovers, but it's a wonder that hearing people do, considering the dumb things they say or do.
- Is there a market for signovers?

The Universal Drum

—a dramatic, visual poem with drum accompaniment

Stage direction: An actor comes on stage rolling a short barrel, tube, and/or a large bowl. A few more people come with a flexible drumhead and use it like a mini trampoline, flinging up some object that's easy to bounce. Another person can bring on the fasteners or whatever is needed to secure the drumhead over the barrel. Some could come in with bongos and tambourines. Others could use their own bodies as drumming instruments (slapping the thighs or chests, clapping hands, stomping the feet, or popping the hand against the open mouth). All of this could be done in a fun, entertaining way. One by one, the ensemble develops an entrancing beat, which leads to a funky dance.

As the dance dies down, members of the ensemble narrate this poem in American Sign Language while others voice in English, perhaps all choreographed to a drumbeat in the background. Specific percussive beats can be used to emphasize or punctuate parts of the poem.

Drum.
(fingerspell)
D-R-U-M.

Musical instrument
of two membranes,
called "heads"
stretched over a frame
lacing binds tightly
over the frame.

37

Drums
found all over the world
since 6000 B.C.
in almost every culture
the most precious of
all musical instruments.

In Africa and Europe,
certain drums symbolize royalty.

In Asia, Russia, and
Native American tribes,
drums are used for ceremonial dances.
In Deaf culture, a drum
is the one musical instrument
that reaches the heart
of a deaf person.

Drums are universal,
creating strength and solidarity,
reflecting the rhythms of life:
the dawning of a new day
the setting of night.

Trees swaying in the breeze.
The rumble of thunderstorms.
A door slamming.
People walking.
Hearts beating.
The rhythms of life.

Strike the instrument
with the hands
and we can create

(Ensemble acts out each of the following creations)

Music
      Rhythms
          Signals
              Marches
                    Dances
                        Conversations.

A drum can express
who you are
and who we are.

I'm deaf and I live
in a Deaf world.

I'm hearing and I live
in a hearing world.

(Deaf and hearing actors, simultaneously)

I'm Deaf and I live   I'm hearing and I live
in both worlds.   in both worlds.

Like the drum
we are
woven together
in one place—

Like the two drumheads fastened
to the frame,
tight,
our hands reach out
to both deaf and hearing worlds.

Using our drum to communicate,
we send our message to you.

(Deaf and hearing actors, simultaneously)

Look   Listen

                    the rhythm of our family

Deaf   hearing

                              equal
                           connected
                            united.

Summer Stock

He sees her in the Yeats poem,
the "glimmering girl with apple blossoms in her hair
who…ran and faded through the brightening air"

Five weeks working closely
on *The Skin of Our Teeth,*
she'll be gone after the show ends

the only one in the cast
with the real desire to communicate with him
When she goes he'll see her
the way she's always been:

pacing, anxious, angry
an ever-present cigarette in her mouth
heading for some unknown territory

Underneath he sees
a red-headed high school girl
who blushes and gets weak-kneed
whenever he looks her in the eyes

Those exotic green eyes, strong cheekbones—
from her Native American great-grandmother—
would go slack, not like an old person's
but a baby's face when finally breastfed

her red-checkered sun dress
hangs loosely on her frame,
the low neckline nonchalantly
exposing a part of her breasts
her white sweat socks crumpled down
revealing her ankles.

He found how she felt about him
at a pool party when she fingerspelled c-r-u-s-h
For weeks she studied a sign language book
practicing in front of mirrors and strangers

On a church parking lot when he touched her
she purred—not by sound but by looks
He kissed her fingers, arms, neck,
watching her upper lip quiver,
amazed at this effect

She's teased as "one of the best actresses
in the country:"
she struts and frets on the stage
she'll flip you the bird or do a jive
with the white man's overbite.
But alone with her in the bathroom,
she's a shy schoolgirl about to get
her first kiss.

He will remember:
the two of them in an inner tube
floating down the Niantic River
her calling him Mr. Testosterone
while he named her Ms. Estrogen

the Christmas lights in her room
how they carry her spirit
wherever she hung them

the way her skirt blew in the wind
as she drove a golf ball
for the first time in her 32 years

the dog following them as they biked to the beach
in a downpour and stopping at the surf
to kiss each other's salty lips and
feel the sand stick to their legs
playing Pac Man at Happy Hollidays'
watching her snap bubblegum
drink O'Doul's while ringing up bonus points

her silver Nova, its old-car odor
and wishing she had taken him
for a joyride along Oceanview Drive

On the last day of the show
he will look at her from the wings as she says
one of the last lines in the play:
"...we have to go on for ages and ages yet."
Then the lights will go down
and this girl who plays Lily Sabina
will go on forever and ever in his mind.

The Liminal Individual

is profoundly deaf—
with an Aussie-like voice
passing for hearing

the hearing take them
for granted and talk
as if they hear perfectly

the Deafies think
they're Hearie wannabes
trying hard
to be the majority:
"hearing-on-the-forehead"
as they would sign

Mother's Day

Along the beaches of Old Lyme
comes a familiar sensation;
an omniscient feeling
with any seashore.

I thought of you, Mother.

The wind and sun playing
with the sea and sand:
running, falling, pushing,
and pulling. A remembrance
of summers past of a mother
introducing her firstborn to
the ocean of life. She would watch:

her deaf boy chase a wave
and race it back

fly with sandpipers
and wave down to her

collect wet seashells
and make her a necklace

erect a castle in her honor
and serve sand crabs for a feast.

She wonders if her son will ever learn
language and form words with his voice.

The man notices the twinkling ripples
and the shore's perfume.
Warm, soft sand envelope his feet.
She was everywhere.

I think of you, Mother.

II. The Falls

I of the Beholder

I lie "unconscious,"
eyes closed,
downstage, facing upstage,
my back two feet from the audience.

I have to be still.
My heart jackhammers,
my breath rattles.

The eye closest to the floor
opens a crack.
The gates in the play open.
All the characters spill out,
one by one.

I fell wrong this time.
All my weight rests
on my left arm, making my
fingers curl involuntarily.
My shin throbs.

I wiggle my toes to make sure
no bones are broken.
They're jammed inside a steel bucket
I stepped into
on purpose.

I blink away the sweat that trickles
into my eyes.

Can the audience see any of this?

Four Haiku

Never in my life
have I seen a toad sit or
put feet on toadstool.

* * * * *

Running, ten below
ev'ry inhale a sharp cut
my lungs are bleeding

* * * * *

Winter in the woods
trees, leaves, lake, sky, squirrels: dead-gray,
even my skin, eyes

* * * * *

coyote bones
scattered along the arroyo
rainstorm to the north

Wallet Photos

His son at two in studio poses
inside plastic frayed sleeves

Nephews Adam and Kyle seven and nine
goddaughter Aidan at eight

all in plastic too—standard school photos

The thick billfold pressed against his rump
reminds him the richness of family

Plus, he's prepared for a time
perhaps stranded somewhere
an uncivilized island

with nothing but his wallet

The Cute Blonde Snake

Skateboarders from all walks of life,
noobs, intermediates, and pros
goofy-footing steezy maneuvers
on their decks in the skatepark:

Ollie-ing
Kick-flipping
Grinding
Board-sliding
Nose-sliding
Mongo-footing
Pop-shuviting
Heel-flipping
Front 180ing
Back 180ing
Half Cabbing
Full Cabbing
Fakie Big-spinning

Then a cute little blonde girl
six years old
wearing a white, sparkly baseball cap
rolls in nonchalantly
on a pink Razor scooter,
snaking around the obstacles
oblivious to all the leaping
testosterone.

Someone's Daughter

a little girl's shoe
lies on the shoulder
of a Kansas highway
once pink now beaten and brown
               where is she

a truck zooms by

the plastic shoe strap
flaps in the wind

Barbershop Fraternities

He just had a nice, old-fashioned haircut
in the oldest barbershop in Arizona.
The barber used a brush that felt good.
One of those 99-cent
plastic pocket hairbrushes
clipped on an advertising board
alongside a picture
of a square-jawed white guy in a crew cut.
He'd seen them in traditional barbershops
ever since he was little and wanted one.

The barber rang it up.
He took out a dollar bill and paid him.
Barber looked at the register, paused.
"Oh, you need 9 more cents for tax?"
"Yeah," he said. "We gotta fee-male guv'nor—
she don't know what's she's doing."

Legal Separation

Oh geez, a wren or some sparrow type of bird built a nest again in that narrow space between the porch light and front wall of my house, obviously she likes the warmth and protective cover which reminds me it was just a year ago in early spring that she or some other bird made that mess with twigs and excrement all over my porch, forcing me to constantly throw away her construction project—three times I had to go out to grab the tuft of grass and toss it out on the lawn and then it so happens that I had to go away for a few days and when I came back there she was sitting comfortably in her new nest…dammit, it has happened all over again, yet this time I just can't muster the urge to disrupt her new family 'cuz every time I go out on the porch to get my morning paper or the mail, she flies away in fear that I would raze her home once again, and so when I get back in the house, she would return to her sitting duty, and then one day my 5-year-old son, whom I can only get every other week, came home from school and mentioned that he hadn't seen the bird in her nest, so I take out a step stool to check and I see she is still there, squatting in her homemade home, frozen with fear, eyeballing me, unsure what to do, so in order to calm her nerves, I slowly back down the ladder and as I step off I see that it's dark outside already, you know, whenever I go outside after dark, she flees the nest but she couldn't fly past the porch cuz she gets confused by the dark and can't escape the confines of the porch ceiling…eventually she settles back in after I go back inside, although it's been a few days now and I have not seen her; you know what's crazy, I had a dream the other night that she left her babies and I could see them poking their little heads above the rim of the nest and the next thing I knew they were in a box on my kitchen table—three eaglets with large curved beaks, wobbling their top-heavy heads; something told me to send a message out on social media asking people what

I should do with them all and that got me thinking immediately of how to feed them and this idea came to get an eyedropper and my son's gecko food—a goopy mango mush.

The last image I had before waking up was squeezing orange liquid down the eaglets' throats while their talons bloodied my fingers.

Crumbs

her
sesame seeds
poppy seeds
rye seeds
pumpkin seeds,
sugar frostings
cheese drippings
muffin morsels
burnt raisins,
bagel pieces…
baked
broiled
toasted
air-fried
scattered black
and brown
in a crumb-catching pan
of our toaster oven—
an eleven-year marriage
all scraped off
in today's
outgoing trash

November Rust

On an early winter night in Boston,
he goes out to his sleeper porch
and looks up at the sky.

Lead-gray clouds race
over the moon, or is the moon
racing behind the clouds?

He thinks of the breakup
with his girlfriend.
Again, he was the initiator.
It's becoming a pattern and
he wants to break it.

He leans against the screen:
the bristles of his beard poke
through into the night.

It hasn't been this warm since 1966,
when the temperature hit a record 75 degrees.

The wind blows through and he smells
a warm August breeze. When it stops,
the screen smells of November rust.

The Perfect Woman

At least once a day
on the balcony of his small-town loft,
he leans against the railing,
watching
the cars go by.

His gaze shifts across the street
to a fancy country store
with an antique wedding dress,
yellowing
in the display window.

It is twilight and the dress
glows white under the track lights.

He feels he is
wasting
his life, waiting.

A Maryland Eastern Shore Life

Salted steamed crabs
spread out on the kitchen table
of my childhood.

Beyond the porch
I see the salt marshes
of my adulthood.

The water falls.

I sit and watch the waterfall
While far from home in Selden Bay
And wonder what's going through
My grandfather's mind today.

Lying beside him,
His loving wife of fifty-five years
Fades before his eyes,
Which well and sting with tears.

Cancer cells multiply and build.
An evil metastasis marches,
Destroys everything under the skin
He so delicately touches.

She will improve, he thinks,
As he force-feeds her applesauce
Tainted with medicine—it may
As well be a spoon of moss.

He's like a child with an old, broken doll,
Trying to fix the legs and arms,
Pushing the stuffing back in,
Not realizing the material has worn.

There is hope.
It's in the hereafter
Just as water runs over the fall.

One Frame at a Time

he died

It's hard to watch my mother go through clips of her life: grey Polaroids of childhood, tattered prints of her parents, her father's army medals, her mother's jewelry

alone on a winter night

She touches each relic and stares, a memory slides in superimposed. She grows still and watches each part of her past.

in his bedroom—

The object is laid back on the table and another is held. One memory segues to the next; her ritual of grief. One day it will be me touching her belongings.

shot himself, my grandfather

Spring

Grandpop Conley died December 3, 1972, heart attack…
walking to his hearse on the way to pick up a body.

Autumn 1970 in high school, Billy Hendricks, the guy I washed
dishes with at the White Coffee Pot—drowned in the Little
Patuxtent River.

At seven an asthma attack killed Eddie Harwell in Summer of '65,
the skinny, arrogant kid from up the street.

Grandmother Borchers passed away. Lymphatic cancer.
She was God in my eyes. July 14, 1986.

My dog, Lucky, was put to sleep after biting a little girl with
leukemia. Fall 1964.

December 11, 1987. Charles M. Borchers, my mother's father, shot
himself in the head in his bedroom on a cold December night in
Westminster.

A cousin, Bobby Conley, died in his sleep from mixing sleeping
pills and alcohol. February 9, 1978.

One of my deaf students at Gallaudet University—who liked *She
Walks in Beauty*—died of a seizure one night in his dorm room.
Gave him a "B" in Literature. Fall of 1992.

The biggest braggart on our floor during my first semester of
college hung himself in the woods on campus. One night a few
weeks before he died, some of us guys snatched a navy-blue ski
cap off of his head and threw it out the window. The cap is still
stuck on a tree limb in the Quad. Summer 1976.

My father's mother, Grandmom Conley, passed on of natural causes. Some of her vital organs pretty much shut down all at once. She loved *Dialing for Dollars* and made the best Maryland crab soup. March 1980.

On April 5, 1994: the birth of my first nephew,
Adam Cole Hartman…Adam of the big blue eyes and the first name of man.

About the Author

Willy Conley's most recent book is *Visual-Gestural Communication: A Workbook in Nonverbal Expression and Reception.* Other books are *Listening Through the Bone—Collected Poems, The Deaf Heart—a Novel, Broken Spokes,* and *Vignettes of the Deaf Character and Other Plays.* Conley is a retired professor of theatre from Gallaudet University, the world's only liberal arts university for deaf and hard-of-hearing students. For more info about his work, please visit: www.willyconley.com.

www.ingramcontent.com/pod-product-compliance
Lightning Source LLC
Chambersburg PA
CBHW031152090426
42738CB00008B/1300